Written by Clive Gifford.
Illustrations by Steve James.
Cover artwork based on designs by Thy Bui.

First published in Great Britain in 2022 by Red Shed, part of Farshore

An imprint of HarperCollins*Publishers*
1 London Bridge Street, London SE1 9GF
www.farshore.co.uk

HarperCollins*Publishers*
1st Floor, Watermarque Building, Ringsend Road
Dublin 4, Ireland

Copyright © HarperCollins*Publishers* Limited 2022

ISBN 978 0 00 856217 5
Printed and bound in the UK using 100% Renewable Electricity at CPI Group (UK) Ltd.
001

A CIP catalogue record for this title is available from the British Library.

Stay safe online. Any website addresses listed in this book are correct at the time of going
to print. However, Farshore is not responsible for content hosted by third parties. Please be
aware that online content can be subject to change and websites can contain content that is
unsuitable for children. We advise that all children are supervised when using the internet.

MIX
Paper | Supporting
responsible forestry
FSC™ C007454
www.fsc.org

This book is produced from independently certified FSC™ paper
to ensure responsible forest management.

For more information visit: www.harpercollins.co.uk/green

AMAZING PUZZLES & QUIZZES

FOR EVERY 7 YEAR OLD

RED SHED

Have fun cracking clues and tackling quizzes with this puzzle book.

You'll find loads of fun questions and exciting brain teasers to challenge yourself with – or you can test your friends and family for hours of fun together!

Along the way, you'll find a mix of all sorts of puzzles – spot the difference, anagrams, quizzes, mazes and more. Each puzzle has instructions at the top of the page that tell you what you need to do. Once you've got your answer, or if you get stuck, head to the back of the book to check the solution.

Lets get started!

Spot the Pair: Strawberry Sundae

Only one of the labelled images on this page is identical to this ice cream – all of the rest have small differences.

Can you work out which image is an exact match?

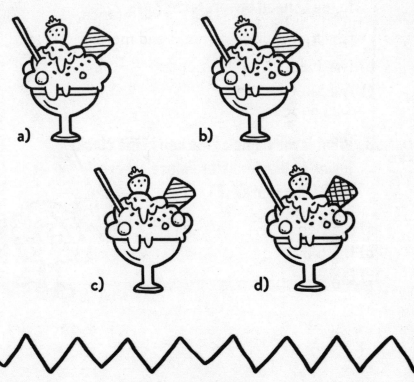

a)

b)

c)

d)

All About London

I. Which of these is the Queen's London residence?

a) Buckingham Palace
b) Palace of Versaille
c) Windsor Castle

2. What nickname is often used to refer to the London Underground?

a) The Pipe
b) The Tube
c) The Shuttle

3. What is the name of the bell in the clock tower of Westminster Palace, where UK Parliament sits?

a) Big Ben
b) Big Billy
c) Big Bob

Anagrams: Weather

Get your umbrella out! Each of these **five types of stormy weather** has had its letters jumbled up. Can you unscramble the letters on each line to spell the words out correctly? A clue is given below each word to help you.

LAHI
Icy balls that fall from the sky

NDIW
Gusts of air

IRDZBAZL
A big snow storm

UNDRETH
The sound caused by lightning

RDOTNOA
A spinning column of air

Planets

1. **Which planet in our Solar System is nearest to the Sun?** *Hint: it shares its name with a Roman messenger god.*

a) Venus
b) Mars
c) Mercury

2. **What is the biggest planet in our Solar System?** *Hint: it is named after the Roman god of thunder!*

a) Earth
b) Jupiter
c) Neptune

RIDDLE TIME!
What is found in MARS, EARTH and JUPITER but not in VENUS or NEPTUNE?

Answers on page 76

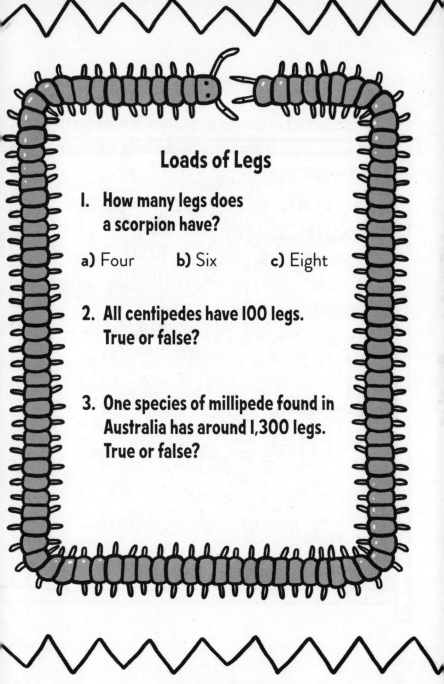

Loads of Legs

1. **How many legs does a scorpion have?**

a) Four   **b)** Six   **c)** Eight

2. **All centipedes have 100 legs. True or false?**

3. **One species of millipede found in Australia has around 1,300 legs. True or false?**

Answers on page 76

Spot the Difference: At the Zoo

Answers on page 76

There are seven differences to spot between the two images below. Can you find them all?

Answers on page 76

Travel Trivia

1. **Which country is famous for the Eiffel Tower, baguettes and Napoleon Bonaparte?**

a) Russia
b) Canada
c) France

2. **Which country do flamenco dancing, Pablo Picasso and tapas all come from?**

a) Spain
b) Malta
c) Italy

3. **Which country contains more of the Amazon rainforest than any other?**

a) The United States of America
b) Uruguay
c) Brazil

Answers on page 77

Make a Match: Jobs

These professional people have lost their tools!
Each tool in the left-hand list matches exactly
one profession on the right. Can you work out
which tool belongs with each person?

Stethoscope	Chef
Hammer	Gardener
Handcuffs	Football referee
Rake	Doctor
Egg whisk	Police officer
Red card	Builder

Sports Day

1. **In athletics, what sport involves jumping over a series of obstacles?**

a) Hurdles
b) Discus throw
c) Relay

2. **What event involves athletes making a hop and a step before leaping into a sandpit?**

a) High jump
b) Triple jump
c) Pole vault

3. **What type of race is run over 42.2 kilometres and is sometimes held in big cities?**

a) Marathon
b) Steeplechase
c) Relay

Answers on page 77

Incredible Animals

1. **Which type of insect can jump around 150 times its body length in a single leap?**

a) Cheetah
b) Ladybird
c) Flea

2. **Only one of these creatures CANNOT breathe through its bottom – which one do you think it is?**

a) Sea cucumber
b) Sloth
c) White-throated snapping turtle

Answers on page 78

Mammal Matters

1. What type of animal is a jaguar?

a) A rodent
b) A big cat
c) A deer

2. What are the only mammals that can fly (not glide)?

a) Possums
b) Hamsters
c) Bats

3. What is the biggest mammal in the world, with a heart around the weight of a car?

a) African elephant
b) Blue whale
c) Grizzly bear

Answers on page 78

4. An African elephant pregnancy lasts for around 22 months, more than twice the length of a human's (around 9 months). True or false?

5. Which of these mammals lives in the icy arctic seas and has a long tusk that can grow up to 3 metres long?

a) Narwhal
b) Dolphin
c) Otter

6. There is a type of camel that always has three humps. True or false?

Answers on page 78

Watery World

I. Which ocean is the biggest in the world, and has a name that comes from a phrase meaning 'peaceful sea'?

a) Pacific
b) Atlantic
c) Indian

2. What are slow-moving rivers of ice on land called?

a) Ice mountains
b) Icebergs
c) Glaciers

3. There is more freshwater than saltwater on Earth. True or false?

Answers on page 78

Unicorn Maze

Can you help the unicorn find a path through this magical maze from the start to the finish?

Raiders and Invaders

I. Which group of ancient people were based in Scandinavia, sailed in longships and fought battles with axes and long swords?

a) Vikings
b) Romans
c) Egyptians

2. Hadrian's Wall was built by the Romans in 122CE and stretches over 100 kilometres. True or false?

3. All Vikings had horns on their helmets. True or false?

Answers on page 79

In Order

Can you put these polygons (two-dimensional shapes) in order of how many edges they have, from fewest to most?

Hexagon

Pentagon

Triangle

Octagon

Square

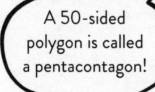

A 50-sided polygon is called a pentacontagon!

Answers on page 79

Word Pyramid I

Below are clues to four words, with the number of letters in the solution given in brackets. Each solution matches the previous line, with one letter added at either the start or the end.

For example, if the first solution was 'AT', the following solution could be 'HAT'.

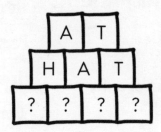

Can you solve the clues to reveal the word pyramid? It might help to jot down the words on a piece of paper.

1. **The opposite of 'off' (2)**

2. **What you get when you take nine from ten (3)**

3. **The quality of a sound (4)**

4. **Another word for a pebble (5)**

Creepy-crawlies

1. How many legs does a spider have?

2. One of these creatures is a long, thin butterfly-to-be, usually with 12 eyes! Which is it?

a) Bee
b) Caterpillar
c) Dragonfly

3. Male stoneflies sometimes do push-ups to impress female stoneflies. True or false?

Funny Stories

1. **Which of these characters from *Alice's Adventures in Wonderland* wears a waistcoat and is often late or in a rush?**

a) The White Rabbit
b) The Queen of Hearts
c) The March Hare

2. **Which character in the *Mr Men* and *Little Miss* books is orange, has very long arms and wears a blue hat?**

a) Mr Greedy
b) Little Miss Brainy
c) Mr Tickle

3. **Which of these is NOT one of the seven dwarfs befriended by Snow White?**

a) Happy
b) Sleepy
c) Chuckles

Answers on page 80

Make a Match: Baby Animals

These baby animals have got lost! Each baby animal name in the left-hand column matches exactly one animal type in the right-hand column. Can you pair them up correctly?

Fawn	**Sheep**
Cub	**Goat**
Kit	**Deer**
Kid	**Ferret**
Lamb	**Wolf**

Mamma?

Unusual Competitions

1. The World Bog Snorkelling Championships are a real competition held every year in Wales. True or false?

2. The town of Oulu in Finland holds a World Championship for playing air guitar each year. True or false?

3. The official sport of Maryland, USA, is jousting on horseback. True or false?

4. There is a World Championship for banana eating held in Edinburgh every year. True or false?

Follow the Line: Knotty Kites

These kites have got their strings all tangled up!
Can you follow the lines to work out which kite
belongs with which child?

Tall Stories

1. **What bird has very large feathers, can grow up to around 2.75 metres tall and run at 70 kilometres per hour?**

   a) Ostrich
   b) Penguin
   c) Roadrunner

2. **Which animal lives in North America, can grow to around 2 metres tall, and has antlers that can be 1.8 metres wide?**

   a) Camel
   b) Moose
   c) Muntjac deer

3. **What part of its body does a giraffe use to clean its nose and grasp leaves?**

   a) Tail
   b) Hoof
   c) Tongue

Answers on page 81

Dino Challenge

Each of these four clues can be answered with a word that can be spelt using only letters found in the word STEGOSAURUS. Can you solve the clues? The number of letters in each solution is given in brackets to help you.

STEGOSAURUS

1. A compass direction (4)

2. The month of the year that comes after July (6)

3. A horned animal, a bit like a sheep (4)

4. A raised platform where plays are performed (5)

Cool Countries

1. **Which of these countries has a maple tree leaf on its flag?**

a) Canada
b) Switzerland
c) New Zealand

2. **Which country is home to the extremely venomous inland taipan snake and funnel-web spider?**

a) The Philippines
b) Australia
c) Germany

3. **Which of these is the name of both a country AND a type of straw hat with a brim?**

a) Paraguay
b) Panama
c) Portugal

Answers on page 82

4. Mumbai's trains carry over 6 million people every day, more than the population of New Zealand. True or false?

5. In which country can you find Mount Vesuvius, a volcano that destroyed the city of Pompeii in 79CE?

a) Italy
b) India
c) Indonesia

Answers on page 82

Captivating Characters

I. **Which character's nose famously grows longer every time they tell a lie?**

a) Rapunzel
b) The March Hare
c) Pinocchio

2. **Which of these characters is known for her VERY long hair?**

a) Snow White
b) Rapunzel
c) Goldilocks

3. **Which famous writer's plays featured the characters of Othello, Hamlet, Titania, Juliet and Miranda?**

Secret Scribbler: Under the Sea

Someone has been up to no good and has scribbled out all the vowels (the letters A, E, I, O and U) from the words below. These are all **animals found in the ocean**. Can you restore the vowels and complete the underwater animals? It might help to jot down the names on a piece of paper.

WH▮L▮

SQ▮▮D

SH▮RK

▮CT▮P▮S

S▮▮H▮RS▮

Where in the World?

1. **If you were looking at the ancient rocks of Stonehenge, which country would you be in?**

a) England
b) South Africa
c) China

2. **If you were swimming next to the Great Barrier Reef, what would be the nearest country to you?**

a) India
b) Canada
c) Australia

3. **If you were standing on the top of Mount Kilimanjaro, what continent would you be in?**

a) Africa
b) Asia
c) South America

Australian Animals

1. **Which Australian creature makes cube-shaped poos?**

a) Emu   **b)** Kangaroo   **c)** Wombat

2. **Which bouncy Australian animal can leap over 9 metres in one bound (longer than a giraffe lying down)?**

a) Wombat   **b)** Kangaroo   **c)** Possum

3. **Which of these foods is a big part of a koala's diet?**

a) Eucalyptus leaves
b) Berries
c) Burgers and chips

4. **Koalas have two thumbs on each paw. True or false?**

Answers on page 83

Riddle Time!

Can you work out the answers to these riddles?

1. What belongs to you but is more often used by your family and friends?

2. What has to be broken before you can use it?

3. What question can you never truthfully answer 'yes' to?

4. What has a tail and a head but no body?

Answers on page 83

Mythical Monsters

1. **In Greek mythology, how many eyes did a Cyclops have?**

a) Five
b) Two
c) One

2. **What monster is said to roam the Himalayan mountain range in Asia?**

a) Yeti
b) Bigfoot
c) Vampire

3. **Which of these creatures is said to live in a Scottish lake?**

a) The Loch Ness Monster
b) The Minotaur
c) Pegasus

Weather Wonders

1. What is the cooling effect of cold moving air on the skin called?

a) Windfreeze
b) Windchill
c) Windnip

2. Approximately how many thunderstorms are happening around the world at any one time?

a) 150
b) 600
c) 2,000

3. Winds on the planet Neptune can reach over 1,750 kilometres per hour – faster than the speed of sound. True or false?

Answers on page 84

Anagrams: Birds

Some birds have got their feathers in a muddle. Can you unjumble the letters on each line to spell out the names of **six types of bird**? The first letter of each word is given in bold to help you.

NAW**S**

OSEO**G**

UC**D**K

WL**O**

NI**B**RO

UTLEUR**V**

Odd One Out: Clown Capers

All of the images on this page are identical to one another – apart from one. Can you work out which image is different to the rest?

Answers on page 85

Incredible Countries

I. **Which country is famed for its banks and watches, and has a population that eats more chocolate per person than any other?**

a) United States
b) Switzerland
c) Belgium

2. **Which European country has around 6,000 islands, including Kos, Crete and Corfu?**

a) Spain
b) Greece
c) Australia

Answers on page 85

Human Body

I. **Where can you find the biggest muscle in your body?**

a) Your chest
b) Your thigh
c) Your bottom

2. **A human's fingernails and toenails grow at exactly the same speed. True or false?**

3. **What handy parts of your body can be found by rearranging all of the letters in the word MARS?**

Answers on page 85

Broken Pieces

Pickles the cat keeps pushing crockery off the shelf! Can you fix these three broken vases by pairing up the pieces that fit together exactly? Each broken fragment fits with exactly one other. The fixed vases should all look like the one on the shelf below.

Food Focus

I. **What's the only fruit with its seeds on the outside of its skin?**

a) Tangerine **b)** Strawberry **c)** Quince

2. **On the Italian island of Sardinia, some people make a cheese containing live maggots. True or false?**

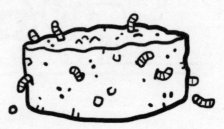

3. **Which type of cheese comes from Italy and can often be found on pizza?**

a) Cheddar
b) Mozzarella
c) Gouda

Anagrams: European Countries

Can you unscramble the letters on each line to spell out **six countries found in Europe**? The first letter of each country is given in bold, to help you.

RN**F**EAC

O**P**LDAN

RENLD**I**A

T**I**YAL

W**S**ENDE

P**S**NAI

Brilliant Babies

1. **Which new-born baby animal can be 1.8 metres tall (as tall as some adult humans)?**

a) Giraffe
b) Rhino
c) Grizzly bear

2. **Which word, beginning with 'c', can mean both a baby cow and a part of your leg?**

3. **Which type of animal can give birth to around 360 babies in its lifetime?**

a) European rabbit
b) Panda
c) Dolphin

Answers on page 86

Mirror Match

Only one of the labelled images on this page is an exact mirror image of this robot – all of the rest have small differences.

Can you work out which image is the exact mirror image?

a)

b)

c)

d)

Super Space

I. **Who was the first person to walk on the Moon?**

a) Buzz Lightyear
b) Neil Armstrong
c) Buzz Aldrin

2. **Humans have sent a car-sized robot to move around the surface of Mars. True or false?**

Answers on page 87

3. Two American astronauts once played basketball on the moon. True or false?

4. What is the name of the galaxy that Earth is found in?

a) The Starry Spiral
b) The Cloudy Trail
c) The Milky Way

5. Which constellation can the star Polaris (also called the North Star) be found in?

a) The Plough
b) The Seven Sisters
c) Sagittarius

6. You can see the same constellations in the night sky wherever you are on Earth. True or false?

Jigsaw: Tremendous Tractors

A piece is missing from this jigsaw! Can you work out which of the puzzle pieces below fits exactly into the empty space on the opposite page to complete the image?

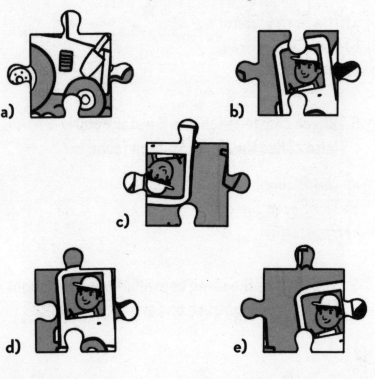

a)

b)

c)

d)

e)

Answers on page 88

Ancient Egyptians

1. **What were the rulers of ancient Egypt called?**

a) Emperors
b) Pharaohs
c) Senators

2. **Ancient Egyptians removed the brains of bodies before they mummified them using a special hook that went up the nose. True or false?**

3. **What is the name of the complex of tombs where King Tutankhamun's tomb was discovered?**

a) The Valley of the Kings
b) The Field of the Dead
c) The Garden of Souls

4. **An ancient Egyptian mummy was wrapped in up to 1,600 metres of bandages. True or false?**

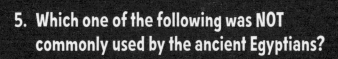

5. Which one of the following was NOT commonly used by the ancient Egyptians?

a) Board games
b) Pens
c) Toothpaste
d) Fireworks
e) Wigs

Mission Impossible

1. **Which of these farm animals can't look straight up at the sky while standing up?**

a) Goat
b) Pig
c) Chicken

2. **Bats are blind. True or false?**

3. **Which of these creatures cannot stick its tongue out?**

a) Crocodile
b) Anteater
c) Giraffe

Answers on page 89

Mole Maze

Can you help the worm find a path through the maze from the start to the finish without being eaten by a hungry mole?

Bird Business

1. **Which bird's young are known as cygnets?**

a) Flamingos
b) Swans
c) Pelicans

2. Which of these birds eats mostly rotting meat?

a) Vulture
b) Starling
c) Pigeon

3. Which of these birds feeds using a long, thin beak, and can fly backwards?

a) Owl
b) Hummingbird
c) Nightingale

Answers on page 90

Anagrams: Ball Sports

Can you unscramble the letters on each line to spell out **six popular sports** you need a ball to play? You might be able to spot some of the relevant balls in the images on this page. . .

BFOLTOAL

GRUBY

RKICTCE

BAVEYOLLLL

NTENIS

OFGL

On the Water

1. **What is the name of the tall pole that rises from the deck of a yacht or ship, which sometimes has sails hanging from it?**

a) Mast
b) Yardarm
c) Jib

2. **What long pole with a blade on the end do rowers use to push their rowing boat through the water?**

a) Rudder
b) Paddle
c) Oar

3. **Which term refers to the right-hand side of a ship, if you are on board and facing forwards?**

a) Starboard
b) Poop deck
c) Rigging

Answers on page 90

Secret Scribbler: Incredible Insects

The secret scribbler returns, and this time they have covered up all of the vowels (the letters A, E, I, O and U) in this list of **six insect types**. Can you work out what vowels are missing to identify the insects?

◆NT

W◆SP

CR◆CK◆T

B◆◆TL◆

B◆TT◆RFLY

M◆SQ◆◆T◆

Pirates!

1. **Which of these is the name of a symbol that many pirates used on the flags they flew from their ships?**

a) The Edward Arms
b) The Skull and Crossbones
c) The Spanish Main

2. **Which of the following was a character in the novel *Treasure Island*, NOT a famous real-life pirate?**

a) Long John Silver
b) Calico Jack
c) Blackbeard

3. **There were never any female pirates. True or false?**

Answers on page 91

Letter Logic

1. Which 'b' can be both a noise made by a dog and the outer layer of a tree trunk?

2. Which 'c' can be both a part of your body and a container for storing treasure?

3. Which 'b' can be both something you use to play cricket and a nocturnal flying animal?

4. Which 'w' can be a movement you make to say hello, or water curling in towards a beach?

Answers on page 91

Word Pyramid 2

Below are clues to five words, with the number of letters in the solution given in brackets. Each solution matches the previous line, with one letter added at either the start or the end.

For example, if the first solution was 'AT', the following solution could be 'HAT'.

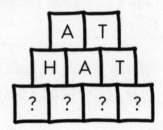

Can you solve the clues to reveal the word pyramid? It might help to jot down the words on a piece of paper.

1. **A word you might use to refer to yourself (1)**

2. **The opposite of 'out' (2)**

3. **A sharp object used in sewing (3)**

4. **To turn quickly in a circle (4)**

5. **Another name for your backbone (5)**

Deadly Dinosaurs

I. Which hunter dinosaur had up to 20 centimetre-long, banana-shaped teeth?

a) Velociraptor
b) T. rex
c) Allosaurus

2. Which dinosaur had three giant horns and a bony frill around its head?

a) Triceratops
b) Stegosaurus
c) Doyouthinkhesaurus

3. Where in the world did dinosaurs live?

a) Just in North America
b) Just in Asia
c) All around the world

Answers on page 92

Awesome Olympics

1. **The Olympic Games began in a town called Olympia – but which country is it in?**

a) Russia
b) Japan
c) Greece

2. **At the Olympics, what type of medal do you get for finishing third in an event?**

a) Silver
b) Plastic
c) Bronze

3. **What is the symbol of the Olympic Games?**

a) Five rings
b) Four squares
c) Seven triangles

4. Athletes at the ancient Greek Olympics took part naked. True or false?

5. What is traditionally carried in a long relay to mark the start of the Olympic Games?

a) A torch
b) A tennis racket
c) An ice cream

Answers on page 92

Milk Matters

1. **Which of these foods does NOT usually contain milk?**

a) Yoghurt
b) Cheese
c) Custard
d) Tofu

2. **In some countries, it was thought that putting a frog in milk would keep it fresh. True or false?**

3. **What nutrient, important for keeping our teeth and bones healthy, can be found in milk?**

a) Potassium
b) Iron
c) Calcium

Follow the Line: Doggy Trouble

These dog walkers have got their leads in a tangle! Can you follow the lines to work out which dog belongs with which dog walker?

The USA

I. How many states are there in
    the United States of America?

a) 24
b) 41
c) 50

2. Which of these landmarks can
    be found in New York City?

a) The Statue of Liberty
b) The Great Sphinx
c) Nelson's Column

3. Which US state can be found in
    the Pacific Ocean, around 4,000
    kilometres from the coast of California?

a) Hawaii
b) Texas
c) California

Secret Scribbler: Fantastic Football

The scribbler is back! This time they have covered up all the vowels (the letters A, E, I, O and U) from these names of **five famous football clubs**. Oi, Ref! Can you work out which vowels are missing and identify the clubs?

T●TT●NH●M H●TSP●R

C●LT●C

L●V●RP●●L

B●RC●L●N●

R●●L M●DR●D

Pet Tests

1. A cat called Stubbs served as mayor of Talkeetna, Alaska, between 1997 and 2017. True or false?

2. Which popular pet is related to the weasel, has been used to protect grain stores from rats, and has a name from the Latin for 'little thief'?

a) Ferret
b) Rabbit
c) Hamster

3. Which of these is NOT a popular breed of dog?

a) Golden Retriever
b) Shiba Inu
c) Norwegian Forest

Answers on page 94

Trains, Trains, Trains

1. What is the name for trains that run on just one single rail?

a) Unirail
b) Monorail
c) Onerail

2. There is a train line in Wuppertal, Germany, that runs upside down, with the train suspended from the track. True or false?

3. The longest railway line in the world can be found in Russia. What is it called?

a) The Baltic Railway
b) The North Eurasian Railway
c) The Trans-Siberian Railway

Vikings

I. **Vikings only travelled within northern Europe. True or false?**

2. **What set of symbols did the Vikings use as their alphabet?**

a) Hieroglyphs
b) Runes
c) Abjads

3. **Some very wealthy Vikings were buried in ships to show their status. True or false?**

4. **What was the name Vikings gave to heaven?**

a) Paradise
b) Valhalla
c) Arcadia

 Answers on page 94

5. Viking longships were just powered by sails, so they could only be used in high winds. True or false?

6. Which Norse god is associated with thunder, and is often shown with a hammer?

a) Odin
b) Thor
c) Freyja

Answers on page 94

SOLUTIONS

Page 5: Spot the Pair: Strawberry Sundae

The matching image is **b**.

a)

c)

d)

Page 6: All About London

1. a   **2.** b   **3.** a

Page 7: Anagrams: Weather

In the order they appear, the stormy weather
words are:
HAIL
WIND
BLIZZARD
THUNDER
TORNADO

Page 8: Planets

1. c

2. b

Riddle Time:
The letter 'R'

Page 9: Loads of Legs

1. c

2. False – centipedes can have over 150 pairs of legs!

3. True – it's called the *Eumillipes persephone*, and has been nicknamed the leggiest animal in the world.

Page 10: Spot the Difference: At the Zoo

Page 12: Travel Trivia

1. c   **2.** a   **3.** c

Page 13: Make a Match: Jobs

The profession/tool pairs are as follows:
Stethoscope – Doctor
Hammer – Builder
Handcuffs – Police officer
Rake – Gardener
Egg whisk – Chef
Red card – Football referee

Page 14: Sports Day

1. a   **2.** b   **3.** a

Page 15: Incredible Animals

1. c   **2.** b

Pages 16–17: Mammal Matters

1. b

2. c

3. b

4. True

5. a

6. False – there are two types of camel, Bactrians (who have two humps) and Dromedaries (who have one hump).

Page 18: Watery World

1. a

2. c

3. False – around 97% of water on Earth is saltwater.

Page 19: Unicorn Maze

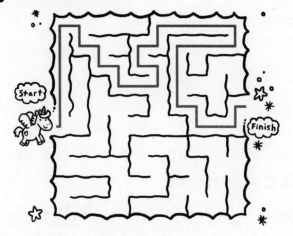

Page 20: Raiders and Invaders

1. a   **2.** True   **3.** False

Page 21: In Order

The correct shape order is:
Triangle (3 edges)
Square (4 edges)
Pentagon (5 edges)
Hexagon (6 edges)
Octagon (8 edges)

Page 22: Word Pyramid I

The word pyramid looks like this:
ON
ONE
TONE
STONE

Page 23: Creepy-crawlies

1. Eight   **2.** b   **3.** True

Page 24: Funny Stories

1. a   **2.** c   **3.** c

Page 25: Make a Match: Baby Animals

The animal pairs are as follows:
Fawn – Deer
Cub – Wolf
Kit – Ferret
Kid – Goat
Lamb – Sheep

Page 26: Unusual Competitions

1. True – competitors aim for the fastest time swimming through a muddy bog.

2. True – competitors rock out on their fake guitars, aiming for the best performance!

3. True

4. False

Page 27: Follow the Line: Knotty Kites

1 with **a**, **2** with **c**, **3** with **b**

Page 28: Tall Stories

1. a   **2.** b   **3.** c

Page 29: Dino Challenge

1. EAST
2. AUGUST
3. GOAT
4. STAGE

Page 30-31: Cool Countries

1. a   **3.** b   **5.** a
2. b   **4.** True

Page 32: Captivating Characters

1. c   **3.** William
2. b   Shakespeare

Page 33: Secret Scribbler: Under the Sea

In the order that they appear, the aquatic animals are:
WHALE
SQUID
SHARK
OCTOPUS
SEAHORSE

Page 34: Where in the World?

1. a   **2.** c   **3.** a

Page 35: Australian Animals

1. c   **3.** a
2. b   **4.** True

Page 36: Riddle Time!

1. Your name!
2. An egg
3. 'Are you asleep?'
4. A coin

Page 37: Mythical Monsters

1. c   **2.** a   **3.** a

Page 38: Weather Wonders

1. b

2. c

3. True – the winds on Neptune are the strongest in our Solar System.

Page 39: Anagrams: Birds

In the order that they appear, the birds are:

SWAN

GOOSE

DUCK

OWL

ROBIN

VULTURE

Page 40: Odd One Out: Clown Capers

The odd one out is **e**.

Page 41: Incredible Countries

1. b   **2.** b

Page 42: Human Body

1. c
2. False. Fingernails grow more quickly than toenails.
3. ARMS

Page 43: Broken Pieces

The pairs are: **b** and **f**, **a** and **e**, **c** and **d**

Page 44: Food Focus

1. b
2. True – it's called *casu marzu* and it's banned in shops!
3. b

Page 45: Anagrams: European Countries

In the order that they appear, the countries are:
FRANCE
POLAND
IRELAND
ITALY
SWEDEN
SPAIN

Page 46: Brilliant Babies

1. a   **3.** a
2. Calf

Page 47: Mirror Match

The mirror image is **a**. The differences in the other images are shown here:

Pages 48–49: Super Space

1. b

2. True – NASA, the American space agency, has actually sent multiple robots to Mars!

3. False – it would be very hard to play basketball on the Moon, as the gravity is so weak! One astronaut did hit a golf ball on the Moon though, in 1971.

4. c

5. a

6. False. The sky looks different depending on if you are in the northern or southern hemisphere.

Page 50: Jigsaw: Tremendous Tractors

The correct piece is **e**. The completed jigsaw looks like this:

Page 52–53: Ancient Egyptians

1. b
2. True
3. a

4. True

5. d – Fireworks were actually invented in China.

Page 54: Mission Impossible

1. b

2. False – it is thought that bats have eyes more sensitive than most humans!

3. a

Page 55: Mole Maze

Page 56: Bird Business

1. b   **2.** a   **3.** b

Page 57: Anagrams: Ball Sports

In the order that they appear, the sports are:
FOOTBALL
RUGBY
CRICKET
VOLLEYBALL
TENNIS
GOLF

Page 58: On the Water

1. a
2. c
3. a

Page 59: Secret Scribbler: Incredible Insects

In the order that they appear, the insects are:
ANT
WASP
CRICKET
BEETLE
BUTTERFLY
MOSQUITO

Page 60: Pirates!

1. b
2. a
3. False – there have been many female pirates over the years, including Zheng Yi Sao, one of the most successful pirates ever.

Page 61: Letter Logic

1. Bark
2. Chest
3. Bat
4. Wave

Page 62: Word Pyramid 2

The word pyramid looks like this:

I
IN
PIN
SPIN
SPINE

Page 63: Deadly Dinosaurs

1. b
2. a. Doyouthinkhesaurus was not a real dinosaur!
3. c

Page 64: Awesome Olympics

1. c
2. c
3. a
4. True
5. a

Page 66: Milk Matters

1. d
2. True – this method appears in Russian folklore.
3. c

Page 67: Follow the Line: Doggy Trouble

1 with **c**, **2** with **a**, **3** with **b**

Page 68: The USA

1. c   **2.** a   **3.** a

Page 69: Secret Scribbler: Fantastic Football

In the order that they appear, the football clubs are:
TOTTENHAM HOTSPUR
CELTIC
LIVERPOOL
BARCELONA
REAL MADRID

Page 70: Pet Tests

1. True　　　　　**2.** a　　　　　**3.** c

Page 71: Trains, Trains, Trains

1. b
2. True
3. c

Page 72-73: Vikings

1. False. They travelled as far afield as North Africa and the Middle East.
2. b
3. True
4. b
5. False
6. b

Try the rest of the series to carry on the fun!